The Man Who Wore Out Mirrors

By

Shaun Maxwell

Dedicated to:

Everyone except Hitler, because Mum said "he wer a bad 'un ".

Other work by Shaun Maxwell can be found on the internet.

Copyright 2015 Shaun Maxwell.

The rights of Shaun Maxwell to be identified as the author of this work have been asserted by him in accordance with the Copyright, Designs and Patent Act of 1988.

All rights reserved: no part of this publication may be reproduced, stored in a retrieval system, or transmitted in any form or any means, electronic, mechanical, photocopying, recording or otherwise without the prior written consent of the publisher or a license permitting copying in the UK issued by the Copyright Licensing Agency Ltd www.cla.co.uk

Book design and lay out by John Winstanley. Pictures by Shaun Maxwell.

Forward:

Since the publication of my book "Unsigned Unscene", Shaun has been a constant supporter of it (...well chapter 9 at least!) and my other work and ideas. He continues to inspire me and others. One day people will realise his genius and I hope that they will not be too late! So, appreciate him now and avoid the rush!

It has been an honour to put together this collection of Shaun's poems and song lyrics….and I know I speak for a lot of others by saying that our lives are more colourful and interesting because we have Shaun "Ali Bongo" Maxwell, in it who does stuff!

John Winstanley. (10th October 2015)

2 x 9

Alright, see you there,
Down on Parody Square,
No gloom rules lie there,
Light my electric chair.
I'm happy as a lamb,
In a world of vegetarians,
Let it glow if you can,
No big goals just little plans.

2 x 9 it's been a long time
2 x 9 I'm doing alright
2 x 9 follow the road sign
2 x 9 now we're doing fine

A6 - scooter boy
Punk girls T shirt says "Destroy"
That was long ago
We're here now let it glow
Be happy if you can
In a tin pot village of the damned
No one understands
A triangular piece of land

2 x 9 see how time flies
2 x 9 But we're doing what's right
2 x 9 love's forever
2 x 9 light up my life
Let it glow

(Dedicated to Miss Garforth)

4 Sheets

The tumbledown we,
A4 sheets
A carousel of beautiful litter
Haunting the streets
No coins of change
Just a strange
Warm summer awash
With shop-bought fodder

Too many comfort zones
Bartered for lost wholes
Too many kickbacks
Each sleeper on the railway tracks
Stained shellac by the passing "click clack"
Of gravy trains that disappear into the black

Oh sometimes my happy souls
Defends the people I behold
In my silent warm
Escape from hole
An open prison
It's not a prison at all - I suppose
You can leave anytime to fight your cause
For the cold careless creature that claws
Needing aspiring wanting all

The tumbling we
A4 sheets
Inkjet FLY Away – a take away
Create -
Demonstrate
To the slavering doubt of control
Just step aside from the road
Remember that "Love" worn so warm

Pass me the dawn
I'm becoming
The person I know
Copyright
On A4

(Thank you Christine).

A picture of Rome

Up there, don't be a square
Or a teddy bear
You're not boring or cute
Life is not an illusion
But why have we grown
To persons unknown?

Scooter-man treads a tarmac trapdoor
Turns the East Lancs Road
To the Via Apia
Mod lives set in the past
Can't go fast
Nostalgia means happier

Infamy, geography
Find a way home
Beautiful people and a picture of Rome

I love to dream
Hepburn scenes
In the grey of the north
Clutch in – speed from apathy
To a picture of Rome.

Almost Classical

A silent maybe,
White walls & corridors,
Did I sense you blushing,
Your eyes touch the floor,
If I know,
What you know,
Then you can be the sun,
As time goes,
Then truth knows,
You will be the one,
What a wonderful feeling I'm down,
The Princess she danced with a clown,
As we sit here absurd in some gothic lament,
Framed by a window,
That's all,
We'll pretend to be statues excluded from time,
It's almost classical

Amy

Amy, Amy, Oh Amy !,
Dry eyed crier,
plots inside her,
Disguised as shyness,
At braced neck speed,
Run rings around the world,
Adorns the predatory fleece,
Dressed solely to appease,
The winds of change,
Are quiet,
Not a word,
Shhhhh ..
The real get things done girl,
She sighs,
Then so bitter sweet,
Says....
"What? Little me?"

Anti Santa Clause

Sowing seeds of greed - you're fishing
the public mood & what they're thinking
the secrets that you just can't buy
extracted from a cold, closed mind
yes I saw what you thought you bought
zero bounces like a naught
markets crash n it's my fault
obscene like a flashers ball

you want to dress my world in rags
deliver babies from plastic bags
schadenfreude politics
a gas price hike for the new Auschwitz
we struggle on, yes we struggle on
keep on swimming but the waters gone
we struggle on, yes we struggle on
can't sink much lower when you're stuck in the mud
so steal the food from under my nose
have your read the anti Santa clause

Avaricious

So delicious,
Avaricious,
Steal the window,
Bleed the light,
Oh so slowly,
Just adore me,
A rich man's war,
A poor man's fight,
Let out the monster from the cage,
Jump around blind, rant & rage,
Never brought to book,
Just burn the page,
Slaughtered in the name of gain,
All the prophets just bring pain,
Sometimes things should never change,
Simple things are set on fire;
Now chained to lust, war & desire,
Peace of mind whored out & tired,
I rip my throat out,
Cannot speak
Cancerous & feeling weak
Sell my body parts too cheap,
To take place amongst the gods
Soul buried deep in permafrost.

Broken Dolls

Here's the man who would be king
Head too big for his shoulders
Gets the doll
Pulls off her arms
Life couldn't get much colder

It's a bit of a girl
Just a slip of a girl
It's a bit of a girl
Just a slip of a girl
I don't believe it
The man who plays with dolls

Here comes that man in uniform
The Emperor's got no clothes on
"Action Man has lost his charm"
Said the terminal plastic orphan

She was a bit of a girl
Just a slip of a girl
It's a bit of a girl
Just a slip of a girl
"It's OUR secret"
The man who plays with dolls

Callahooli man

Bore out of the silent bog
Floated east lashed to a log
Lands close to dawn -
To peat-stained, salt-glazed fog.
Dressed in paraffin rags
Incendiary spirit soaked - clogged.
Bitter history stuck between fangs -
That bit winter as the church bells rang.

"Hide the children, the Callahooli man comes
He'll strike you all deaf and dumb"
All that is left is residual sight –
Benign horrors that stalk in the night.

With Guernica further
His claws dig in farther
Levels the mountains
Swallows up wives!
Till his dark sated eyes
Rule over his victims
The people move on
Run, run for your lives!

Devouring the past
The then until now,
Restless and hungry
Pushing the hours;
'Til all that is gone
Is empty and blind
The Callahooli man
Has eaten up time.

CANUTE

Why are we waiting?
What are the traffic lights stating?
Invisible people into 9 to5 freefall
I'm tired of waiting for you.
As I try to get at the truth.
Soaked with emotion
It's time to move on
Angels & devils on many levels
Disguised as crosswords clues
Is it wise to be totally nude?
Jokes are just tokens
My life in nuance?
I'll watch the sky fall
Turn back the tide? ... No!
I'm wired to the fate of a fool
And I'm tired of playing Canute.

Christmas Turkeys part 1

Ho ! Ho ! Ho !,
Slade jukebox gropes ,
Booze,
Works do's ,
Mistletoe,
Beergoggled offensive blokes,
Repeating cheap shit cracker jokes,

Kissing the frog
In the bog
Encountering a Christmas log,
Sambuca pukes the flames of shame,
Tell the boss he's fucking gay,
So you're heading for a seasonal fall,
We're Christmas turkeys, one & all'.

Chuckies Song

Chuckie was an usherette,
Choc ice sticking from my neck
Boycey slowly cast his net facsimile psychopath of love...
Twins of Evil Cinema - Nazi memorabilia
Cine 8 - Mushroom head
Long knives and the psychopath of love
(Break)
It all comes to a sticky end ... Psychopath of .....
LOVE!

Duvet Lover

Fuel bills my only fuel,
Body warmth & the duvet lover,
Shiver,
I'm the embryo of poor,
No food in old Mother Hubbard's cupboard,
Shudder,
Thank God it's pay day tomorrow.
King for a day,
This waif's astray,
My dock end search is over,
Till then I'll split a cig,
And retreat beneath my duvet cover.

Fabric

I relived in the scent,
A childhood smell,
Of sheets & pillows,
A cuddle jumper,
A security blanket,
Comfort,
A fabric conditioner,
Our past,
Now I'm doing her laundry ,
Trying to keep busy,
Praying for Mum

The Extra

I'm the extra has been
In every Cinemascope movie
On the periphery….
I remained unseen
Till widescreen TV

Kaput

Empty
Disposable
Plastic
Lighter
You're
Dead
To
Me.
Capisce ?
Kaput

Haircuts pt 1

Childhood haircuts
Zigzag fringe
I'm an outcast
Broke & shamed
In the kitchen
With any luck I'll escape with a Friar Tuck
Dad's the barber
 'Oh my God!'
A pissed up Irish Sweeney Todd
'Wet your hair'
Oh dear me
That means shrinkage guaranteed
Hack, hack, hack at the back
Chunky clumps of hair like flak
Sad little birds' nests fall to earth
No nits for chicks just a dandruff shirt
"The bowl's too big!"
Sigh of relief
My reprieve is very short & brief
Now Dad's addled master plan
Means one thing only
That damn pan
The one that cooked the veg for Mum
Now I'm the cabbage overdone
Blunt scissors gnaw into my brain
I'll never be the same again!

Lazarus Unchained

The summer of sandy love,
Washed up & blew away,
Our footsteps disappear,
Dissolved into the waves,
The coffee coloured sea,
Absolved me from within,
Your ever-changing moods,
Lithe like plasticine,
Five times twice as nice,
Nine times blown away,
Ring out the leper bells,
Lazarus unchained,
Bring out the dancing girls,
Turn up the background noise,
Welcome to my world,
Of sad & broken toys.

Leafless

Leafless in the Garden of Eden
Mighty mighty mighty mighty fall
Houston we've got a problem
See Gagarin's children in the hall
Show me who I am
Show me who I am
I'm a Taser Puppet
Hanging like a puppy XX eyed
Leaves are on trees
Waiting for an autumn breeze
Leafless in the Garden of Eden

Icy icy icy icy balls
Houston got a problem
Mighty mighty mighty mighty fall
Show me who I am
Show me who I am
We all go stand in line
Waiting for the first time
Get up early, spank the monkey
'Cos I'm the apple of your eye
Show me who I am
Show me who I am
Oh I'm a Taser Puppet
Hanging like a puppy XX eyed
We all go stand in line
Waiting for the very first time

Lemon Lips

Lemon lips ,
Twisted slice of life,
Supping schadenfreude cocktails,
Bigging up - putting down,
Climbing the ladder breaking the rungs,
Wanking venom on victims castrated in slums,
Relish the rumour,
All sense is self,
Wronging the rights,
For everyone else.

Bitter & twisted never tasted so good,
With a stroke of a pen,
The safety net's gone,
You're all lazy bastards,
You're all drunken, whores,

You're dishonest scroungers...
'Well no I'm just poor!'
Would be my answer,
If I had a voice,
Would be my answer,
If I had a choice

Your words boldly echo,
In each empty ward,
Nursed by contractions
Till no one cares anymore.
So don't give me more scapegoats,
This is class war,
You really do hate us,
We're common as muck,
Breeding like rabbits,
And don't care a fuck,
So it's time to teach us degenerate strays,
Bring back the old order,
Know your place,
A cap-doffing public,
Repeating your lies,
Quoting your medias,
Perpetual tripe

Flat screen riots,
Immigrant scum,
DWP holidays for the work-shy bums,
The bollockless puppets,
Continue your work,
The rapacious & greedy dish the same dirt,
Empathy's dying it's a bit of a chore,
Make no bones about it ,
This is Class War.

Limbo

I can't find the words anymore
To risk all & be brave
On the edge of limbo
I really want to know
But I'm scared of your thoughts
My tumbleweed questions
Could be you've gone to seed - No!

A frosted glass ghost land
Staring at phones
A "How far?" text
"Are you at home?"
A "Can I ring you?"
"But are you busy tonight?"
Don't want to seem pushy
But I miss you "alright!?"

Lion Tamer

Crack, crack …down, down,
'Til eyes are empty ,
No more proud,
No carrot just stick,
Just fear, no prick,
The Lion tamer's back in town,
Takes your dreams & keeps them bound.

Love is blind

Since I went blind,
How lucky I've been,
You've never changed,
The eternal teen,
As I grow old in your failing sight,
To me you look as you did,
In the prime of your life
But do I repel you in physical love?,
I know your body's now softer,
Like your gentle voice,
In the years bound together,
Since I first saw your face,
To the eyes of a blind man,
You've never changed,
I am so lucky,
I bless that day.

Master of the Atom

Left & right one o'clock drunks
Late night lock-up morphine monks
Scream the head butt thumpin' walls
A mother load on overdose
In & out of consciousness
I don't care no more or less
Touching Darwin's interface
No more collective - disintegrate

Escape the dark – I'm Master of the Atom
Right at the start – I'm Master of the Atom

And I'm fleeing deep inside
Breathing, bleeding pure light
A shapeless star
I'm Master of the Atom

MRS SPIDER'S GHOST

I killed a spider
"Thank you" said the fly.
"Now I'm going to buzz you,
Night and day, day & night".
"Did you ever think of them spiderettes?"
"Motherless in life"
"I came to offer my feeble self"
The ultimate sacrifice
I fled into the garden
When another voice in turn said
"You'd better be cremated!" lisped an angry worm
"For when you die we'll find you
No peace in death...you'll writhe
We'll bore into your clothing
So all can get inside".
Now through my act of violence
I'm haunted for all time
"Quite right!" said Mrs Spider's ghost
"Indubitably." said Mr Fly.

One

One step away from
You
Cool
Suicide
Youth
Happiness
Friendship
Poverty
Proof
Lying
Crying
Smiling
Gloom
Two steps back
One closer to you
Selfish
Introvert
Extrovert
New
Life
Death
Breathless
Truth
Acting
Fame
God
("Who?")
Two steps back
To dream anew
One more step and I become you.

Ode To Snow:

Bugger off Snow ...no one wants you,

It's spring you icy bastard...

We've got things to do

TOAST

With my satirist knife
I cut the egg,
Spilling the dregs
Of yoke and cell,
Along with words,
The politic shell,
Slimes sideways slide
To the left
To the right,
In words,
Fragmented,
Pageward.

Partners in clay

What do they say?
We're partners in clay
She looks over my shoulder all the time
Flat broke are we
Just pennies to see
Melt into each other's line of sight

Why do friends weep?
On my frozen cheek
And give us dead flowers lily white
Why do they cry?
Transferring denial
Saying "Maybe it'll be better next time"

There is no wild wind or that kind of thing
Just the seasons passing by
Here comes summertime again
Marbled autumn splashing rain -
Snow to ice then on to Spring
Years are such trivial things
Eternal overlap we twine

In heavens above
Unquestioned love
Bound circles blissfully so blind
No miss you or shame
No loss or pain
Our ghosts cost physical decline

Together again not partners in clay
My love is yours and yours is mine
In the summertime again
Laughing tumbling unconstrained
It's really summertime this time.

People, States & Parties

Come & buy my noise
"Heavens to Murgatroyd!"
Kazoos, balloons, buffoons in my head
My spiritual existence
I am lead
Bela Lugosi's dead
That's what Bauhaus said
I thought I saw him in ASDA buying bread
But I was mistaken
'Sorry Fred'.
Let's talk a while
You have to smile
When the bad ones gone away
Let's stalk a while
You run a mile
But I think I'm going to stay

Soaking up garbage
People, states & parties
Chewing the carpet
People, states & parties
White mice on steroids
Crap gangsters saying 'Boids'
A la di Dali Dada-painted shed
My lyrical ineptness badly read

Poetry crimes

Hackneyed love explodes
Like a boil on the devil's behind
Septic, grows uncertain
Bad talk seeps from kind
Where once I would have kissed it
A sulphur smell ignites
Troubled tummy rumbles
From where the sun once shined
Twenty tortured poets
Cliché ridden souls
Once took us to heaven
Now dig us a hole
With every sating spadeful
Down and down we go
You'll find us in the pits of Hell
Literally shoveling coal
Defy the imagination
A chance to let off steam
To burn loves candle at both ends
To torch the book of dreams
Much comfort in morbidity
It dampens happy times
Beauty is uncertain
Denied in poetry crimes.

Ponders End?

Between pen & paper

There's a wasteland

Scream

Scream children, scream!,
Scream against the past,
The burned,
The words,
Perpetuating hurt,
That keeps the present shallow,
In sanctuaries hollow,
Where each lie takes its turn,

Scream children scream!,
Scream against the fake dawn,
The lies,
The trials,
Meanwhile,
The same old same old faceless,
In bargain bucket basements,
Play 'Twister' boy it hurts,

Scream children, scream,
Scream for new tomorrows,
See truth,
See through,
High on expectations,
Rise above stag nations,
Be an angel when you burn.

Serial killer

Yes, I took a shine to him,
He was calm, friendly – inviting conversation,
Walked with a slight limp,
Bearded reservation,
An E(a)ves eye boy ,
Affable, amenable - point taken..believable,
Something dangerous lurked,
Between that well pressed shirt,
A smile that never gave away a thing,
A disarming , charming – insignificance,
Like a serial killer,
In all his magnificence

The Girl Who Untied Knots (For Alex)

I can't do it "Aaaagh, you do it!" ,
"Give it here", she says,
Taking the laces.
"You've got no patience
Men, I don't know!"
In a mock distressed tone,
"Hope not", thinks I - whoa!

Slowly, methodically,
Over and under,
Twisting turning,
Above then below.
"Sorted", she says,
With the smile of a victor,
I love it, as she twist me around her little finger
Then "that's what I'm here for!"

Shadrach Black

He loves it – Owns it,
The coat of Wilfred Owen,
Possessing powers in words of ghosts,
Wrapped up tightly,
A world's poetic nightmares,
The magic powers of an Army surplus bloke.

Oh no! Someone's stolen his hope,
Shadrach Black wants his coat back
Oh no! some scumbags idea of a joke
Shadrach Black wants his coat

Now he's lost his roots,
No Dead Shot Keen for Billy's Boots,
Alf Tupper's chips are overcooked,
He's under pressure Gollum's lost his precious,
So he haunts the streets of Manchester

Slow Death by Karaoke

Someone decided to kill my favourite song
But I'm a meticulous man
The good the bad the ugly sing along
No one can ruin a classic
Like a fan

(Chorus)
La la la la la la
Slow death by karaoke
La la la la la
Slow death by karaoke

Pop Pop Pop stars in their eyes
I'm a peculiar guy
The good the bad the ugly sing along
They just follow the words
Follow the words
Follow the words

(Chorus)

The Hoy Beardy Rant

Hoy beardy!
Where's the bonfire?
To burn your poetry look
Your acoustic guitar
That drones like a fart
Gutless with no hook.
Don't try to entice me to your

Hippie-framed world
Liberate through drugs
Sordid social comment
Sat at home so smug.
It's an armchair revolution
Middle classly vague
A trivial token spoken
With the passion of inane.
Miss out If's and But's
When juggling with faux pain
Hoy beardy,
Where's the bonfire – of vanity
So lame.

The Man Who Wore Out Mirrors

Trace the outline beautiful face
Your waistline hates your dinner
It's not a look just a matter of taste
Not everyone's a winner

A narcissistic sinner
The Man Who Wore Out Mirrors
And you're posing like a real cool killer
The Man Who Wore Out Mirrors

Kitsch beyond compare
One single grey hair
That sticks out like a rope
Peter Pan is growing old

A narcissistic sinner
The Man Who Wore Out Mirrors
And you're posing like a real cool killer
The Man Who Wore Out Mirrors

Oi! So yer gawpin' at nowt
Yer sprawsin' sprawsin sprawsin about
Oi! So you just worked out
Yer fawnin' fawnin' & I'm sick of it...Sick of it!

Deep as a puddle & twice as wide
An absolute beginner
I wish that you were Dracula
So the mirror couldn't see ya

A narcissistic sinner
The Man Who Wore Out Mirrors
An absolute beginner
The Man Who Wore Out Mirrors

13

When you were one,
I was 13,
Held you close,
Promised never to let you go

When you were 5,
I was 13,

We played house,
Domestic dreams

When you were 10,
I was 13,
Cartoon characters,
Buffoonery

Now you're 16,
I'm still 13,
Too grown up,
To play with me

All my children,
Eventually leave,
I let go,
My promise broke

Toast

"You ok?" she says
"Breakfast?"
"Yeah",
As she clanks down the plate,
"Look I'm sorry I got in so late"
She gave me a hug,
With all the burnt toast warmth of over egged love.

Washing Machine

Washing machines make things clean,
I want a massive washing machine,
Chuck in war, stress, politicians & death,
My Washing machine would make the world clean.

Shaun Ali Bongo 11/08/14

Watchman

I am the Watchman
A starry eyed 4 year old
Weeping out tears too old
The one & only truth
I am the watchman
When you're down
When you're down
It will be worth it if you stick around
Because I love you
Because I love you

[Chorus]
And in the morning
When you wake up
My work is done
So I disappear
With all your fears
I am the Watchman
I have no option

I am the Watchman
An incidental shadow
Forever is just tomorrow in the eyes of youth
I am the Watchman
In your eyes I'm only me
But I'll show you what really lies beneath
If you promise not to leave
If you believe
I love you
I love you
(Chorus)

Shaun Ali Bongo 10/12/2014

YES

Light eats dark,

Love destroys hate,

Fill up your life,

Inhabit the waste,

Plant seeds of hope,

Bring dignity's grace,

So your smile kills the frown,

With a beautiful –

……. **Yes**

Chapter 9: The Penniless Playboy.

From "Unsigned Unscene" by John Winstanley.
Edited and reproduced with the author's consent.

People never cease to disappoint me. Mostly I feel under whelmed by their lack of originality or being brave enough to be different. But I suppose that has always been the case. The recycling of dirge and fashion speeds up every time. A new fad, maybe flavour of the moment or seconds of fame instead of the Warholian 15 minutes is appropriate today — and less so tomorrow. Everyone creates their own truth but some are more honest than others and these are usually the lepers and outcasts. Nobody wants their bubble burst but I wonder who's blown it in the first place and I mean that in more ways than one. Someone once said "Music's not that important you can eat it"— that's because most of it is shit!

Made in the USA
Monee, IL
03 May 2026

49437983R00024